easy world craft

Flower Arranging

easy world craft

Flower Arranging

A handy step-by-step guide

Mark Welford and Stephen Wicks

LONDON, NEW YORK, MELBOURNE,
MUNICH, DELHI

Project Editor Katharine Goddard
Senior Art Editors Glenda Fisher, Elaine Hewson
Managing Editor Penny Smith
Senior Managing Art Editor Marianne Markham
Jacket Creative Nicola Powling
Pre-Production Producer Rebecca Fallowfield
Senior Producer Charlotte Oliver
Art Director Jane Bull
Publisher Mary Ling
Special Sales Creative Project Manager Alison Donovan

DK INDIA
Managing Editor Alicia Ingty
Editors Janashree Singha, Manasvi Vohra
Senior Art Editor Balwant Singh
Art Editor Zaurin Thoidingjam
Assistant Art Editor Nikita Sodhi
Managing Art Editor Navidita Thapa
Pre-Production Manager Sunil Sharma
DTP Designers Satish Chandra Gaur, Rajdeep Singh

First published in Great Britain in 2014
by Dorling Kindersley Limited
80 Strand, London WC2R 0RL

Material in this publication was previously published in:
Flower Arranging (2011)

A Penguin Random House Company

Copyright © 2011, 2014
Dorling Kindersley Limited

2 4 6 8 10 9 7 5 3 1
001 – 193363 – June/2014

A CIP catalogue record for this book is available
from the British Library

ISBN 978-1-4093-6924-0

Printed and bound in China by Leo Paper Products Ltd.

Discover more at **www.dk.com/crafts**

CONTENTS

INTRODUCTION

Stephen (right) and I opened our shop, Bloomsbury Flowers, in London's Covent Garden, which is close to the Royal Opera House where we both danced many times.

As with ballet, technique is all-important in floristry. Learning how to arrange flowers in a hand-tied bouquet was one of the first skills we had to master.

We met in 1970 in London at White Lodge, the Royal Ballet Lower School, and although we were a school year apart we became friends. In the late 1970s we joined the Sadler's Wells Royal Ballet, which was later to become known as the Birmingham Royal Ballet.

As we neared our "sell-by date" as dancers in the 1990s, we discussed what we would do when we retired. Stephen has always loved flowers and had already arranged the flowers for a friend's wedding. Although I was a keen gardener, I knew little about the world of cut flowers, so it was somewhat of a surprise when Stephen suggested the idea of opening a flower shop together: "All we need are some buckets, a cold tap, and a pair of scissors!"

We applied for support from the Dancers' Career Development (DCD), a charity that helps ex-dancers make the transition into a new career. With the DCD's generous support, we were able to open the doors of Bloomsbury Flowers in Covent Garden in December 1994. We made a promise to ourselves that we would not compromise on the quality of our flowers, but also ensure that they always provide the best value.

Our mission is to make our flowers as theatrical as possible while following our motto of "less is more" by ensuring that even the simplest bunch of tulips leaves the shop looking exquisite, unpretentious, and beautifully wrapped. We are always confident that once a customer removes the wrapping, the flowers will still look fantastic. We have even managed to change the style of the presentation bouquets handed to ballerinas at the end of a performance at the Royal Opera House, London: we have created a unique way of wrapping the flowers so they are not encased in cellophane (which reflects the stage lights so the flowers can't be seen) and can be enjoyed by the audiences, too.

Our ballet background has provided us with some invaluable experience when it comes to floristry. Timing was a fundamental part of our preparation and performance on stage every night, and we have since found that timing is an important aspect of being a successful florist. For example, we are always aware of how long it takes to make up a hand-tied bouquet, install arrangements throughout a hotel, and prepare flowers for an event so they will look their best. We also know that good technique is fundamental to being a confident ballet dancer – and the same is true for floristry. In this book you will learn valuable basic techniques that will enable you to make all the arrangements featured, and inspire you to try creative designs of your own.

We have taken time to decide which designs we should include in this book; they're inspired not only by life, but by things that you may find in your own home. We have also focused on surroundings, colour, and containers, as these are all essential elements to consider when putting together an arrangement. Being aware of the environment in which the flowers will be positioned is important: what works well in opulent surroundings will not necessarily look as good in a venue with a minimalist look. Colour is of paramount importance, and one aspect of floristry that can be a little overwhelming; it's important to know how to work with colour in your designs. We have learnt from each other over the years, as Stephen, if left to his own devices, prefers to work in tonal colours, whereas I always lean towards mixed colours. Containers, too, play a vital part in floral design, and over the years we have built up a large collection. They range from clear vases and galvanized buckets to wooden boxes tied with seagrass, antique wine crates, jewellery boxes, coloured glass containers, and stoneware containers, many of which you will see through the book.

The aim of this book is to inspire, not intimidate, and we hope that our style will become your style, too. Whether it involves learning a simple technique to arrange single blooms in a container or using insider tips to create a large-scale display, this book is about making what is already beautiful even more so.

The interior of the shop is our stage, and the set changes almost daily with deliveries of fresh flowers and foliage. We love the way flowers can instantly transform an environment.

We believe that attention to detail and presentation is everything; our simple but stylish packaging for our flowers allows them to speak for themselves.

PRINCIPLES

This section explains everything you need to know to pick the right flowers in the most suitable colours, prepare and arrange them skilfully, and position them for the best effect.

LESS IS MORE

Our philosophy is all about "less is more". There is no need for complicated tricks and overpowering displays to make your flowers look good; often, the simplest of arrangements can have the most wonderful impact. To make fantastic flower arrangements, you just need to follow some simple rules and think about how to be more creative with, for example, the mixed bunch of flowers that you have bought from a limited selection on sale, or gathered from your garden. Rather than following the standard approach of putting the flowers straight into a vase together, the different elements can be separated into individual containers so that each becomes a beautiful statement in itself.

MIXED FLOWERS

Roses and gypsophila are typically sold and arranged together. It's not wrong to do this, but it doesn't show either variety of flower at its best. The fluffy gypsophila doesn't enhance the dense, compact rose petals in the right way, and together they look rather unexciting and dreary.

THEORY

CREATIVE SOLUTION

By separating the two varieties of flower and placing them in different containers, the gypsophila becomes a delicate cloud of tiny flowers that has an airy, dreamy quality while the deep, rich tones of the red roses resonate together to look exquisite – our "less is more" theory.

SPACE

Before you even think about choosing a container, a colour scheme, and flowers and foliage, consider the space in which you will position your arrangement. When we are asked to design flowers for an occasion – be it for an office or entrance hall, a formal dinner, an intimate hotel room, or a wedding party – we always visit the venue first if we are unfamiliar with the surroundings. We need to make sure that we understand the proportions of the room, and exactly where the flowers will be placed.

WIDE

If you have a large, spacious room to work with – perhaps a grand entrance area, or a large reception room, where the flowers may be seen from several sides – one big, all-round statement piece will work much better than a few small, insignificant displays. Choose a substantial vase or container and fill it with an abundance of lush, opulent, seasonal flowers. It's also worth thinking about what the arrangement will stand on: a plinth or side table will influence how tall the flowers and foliage should be.

NARROW

A windowsill, mantelpiece, desk, or shelf may seem a difficult spot to fill with flowers, but a container filled with bulbs or potted herbs will suit the space perfectly. This type of design will also be long-lasting, as bulbs and herbs with roots will grow well if there is enough natural light in the room.

LOW

It is important to remember that people need to see each other above the flowers if you are designing an arrangement for a coffee table or as a table centrepiece for an office meeting room or a dinner table. Choose low arrangements – simple designs often work best – and make sure the flowers complement the container. The flowers will also last longer, as their stems will be short.

TALL

A tall arrangement will create the right impact if you are working in a high-ceilinged room, an entrance hall, or need to draw the eye upwards. Displays for this space work best if they are not overly fussy, so keep them quite minimal, striking, or architectural in design – perhaps with just a few carefully chosen flowers.

COLOUR

Perhaps the most powerful component of any flower arrangement is its colour scheme. Colour is emotive because it has an immediate impact on our senses, and it can communicate a mood or a message almost instantly. There is a spectacular array of colours in nature – from subtle, harmonious tones to striking, intense, iridescent hues – and flowers encapsulate much of that dynamic range and diversity. Some basic principles about colour theory can be applied to flower arranging to help you choose the right flowers and foliage to make designs that create an inviting atmosphere and are stylish to look at.

COLOUR THEORY

In colour theory, the three primary colours – red, blue, and yellow – can be mixed in different combinations to create a spectrum of other colours. These combinations are arranged in a simple circle, or colour wheel, to show their relationship to each other. This colour wheel (right), composed of flowers and foliage, shows how these relationships work in practice.

WHAT WORKS

Colours that lie near or next to each other on the colour wheel contain elements of the primary colours they sit between, so they go well together. For example, purple harmonizes well with blue and red because it sits in between them on the colour wheel. Each colour also has a tonal value – a light and dark version of that colour – that also creates harmony, but can influence the mood of an arrangement to make it warm or cool, or gentle or intense. So pale purple, blue, and pink blooms convey a light, gentle mood, while strong, darker tones of these colours are more intense and dramatic. Foliage, with its different textures and subtle variations of green, also helps different colours to blend well.

Flower Colour Wheel
This colour wheel reveals how colours influence each other when they are placed near, next to, or opposite each other.

Primary colours
Red, one of the three primary colours, sits equidistant from the other two primary colours, blue and yellow, on the colour wheel. They are the key anchors of the colour wheel and, mixed together in different proportions, they create all other colours.

Harmonious colours
Colours that sit next to or near each other on the colour wheel, such as pinks and purples, make a visually pleasing combination when arranged in a mixed display.

Contrasting colours
Colours that sit directly opposite each other on the colour wheel are known as complementary, or contrasting, colours, as they appear more powerful together than they do apart. For example, blue and orange flowers enhance one another when mixed together in a design.

Colours that sit opposite each other on the colour wheel have a powerful effect on one another. In nature, some complementary colours enhance each other, and can look better together than apart. For instance, the flowers in a red and green design, or a pink and lime-green bouquet, look more vibrant, saturated, and pure when placed together than if arranged separately.

THE RULES IN PRACTICE

Although there are not necessarily any colours that shouldn't go together, some combinations work better than others. For example, yellow and orange are a good combination, as are purple, red, and pink. A good guideline is to limit yourself to three or four harmonious colours or two complementary colours; a multicoloured arrangement can impair your visual pleasure, as it is too confusing on the eye. It's also worth bearing in mind that a mass of one variety of flower in just one colour can create more impact if it is arranged well. Before you buy any flowers, look at the space in which you will position your arrangement and think about which flower colours go best with the colour scheme of your surroundings so you can create the most pleasing impact.

USING WHITE IN ARRANGEMENTS

White flowers should be used carefully in arrangements because white can dominate some colours and dull others. White and red, for example, are both hard colours that can jar together; we prefer to use cream and maroon flowers that, when teamed with foliage, make a softer, more luxurious mix. However, we often use white flowers on their own or with green foliage, or we combine them with cream blooms, which soften and enhance them. And when teamed with a limited palette of harmonious colours, such as blue, purple, and green, white flowers can take on an almost iridescent, shimmering quality amid the other blooms.

ESSENTIAL CONTAINERS

Every flower design must suit the occasion and the surroundings it is intended for, so decide on your container first before you select the flowers: think about the impression you want to create and consider the size, shape, and colour of the container in order to get the right look. This selection of vases represents the four essential shapes you need in your collection; with this limited choice you can create a wonderful variety of arrangements and show off the flowers to their best effect.

FISH BOWL

This globe shape is good for highlighting the beauty of just a few blooms by curling and swirling them within the curved contours of the bowl. It is also ideal for displaying tall-stemmed hand-tied bouquets that require a dramatic edge.

CUBE VASE

A square-shaped vase is perfect for displaying a mass of one type of flower, and ideal for smaller, compact arrangements with short-stemmed flowers. The straight sides of this vase enforce a geometric framework onto the blooms, giving them a modern look.

COLUMN VASE

A straight-sided vase such as this can "contain" the flowers within it, so you can use it to create sculptural or uniform arrangements. Its extended height allows displays of tall-stemmed flowers to be well supported so they don't droop, but you can also use it for contemporary designs, such as a compact ball or "bomb" of large, domed flowers that sits on the rim of the vase.

FLARED VASE

This vase allows flowers and foliage to fall naturally at pleasing angles to create a fan shape, and it can display a wide variety of flowers clearly in a large arrangement. Its tapered base also limits the spread of their stems, ensuring that any displays requiring an extravagant flourish or an element of drama or impact have added height.

CONTAINERS FOR EVERY OCCASION

This selection shows something of the variety of colours, textures, shapes, and sizes of vases and containers that can inspire your flower design. Choose a container that lends itself to the flowers, and vice versa. Any non-watertight containers can be adapted using cellophane or cut-down plastic water bottles. If you can't find the right container, you always have the option of using floral foam (pp38–41) or arranging the flowers as a hand-tied bouquet (pp34–37).

ORANGE FISH BOWL ↓
Neon-coloured globe-shaped glass vase, best used for modern domed flower designs.

EPHEMERA VASE →
Column vase covered in old, torn papers to create texture and interest with a mixed selection of flowers.

↓ PINK FLOWERPOT
Flared glass vase that lends a modern air to a simple small vase arrangement.

↓ METAL VASE
Classic version of a flared vase that suits traditional displays.

↑ SMALL BUCKET
Modern galvanized bucket that looks great with a mass of one variety of short-stemmed blooms.

MINI CUBE ↑
Tiny version of a cube vase for individual blooms.

TARTLET TINS ↑
Use as place settings with short-stemmed single flower heads.

CONFIT CAN ↑
Empty can makes an attractive flared vase for a potted bulb.

↑ COCONUT SHELL
Treat like an opaque fish bowl for minimal, modern displays of exotic blooms.

↑ METAL URN
Use for miniature versions of flared vase displays with a classic selection of mixed flowers.

OPAQUE COLUMN VASE ↓
Patterned column glass vases in neutral colours look good with just a few long-stemmed statement flowers.

POTTERY VASE ↓
A patterned, flared vase shows off most flower arrangements well.

TERRACOTTA CUBE ↓
Non-porous container has a cut-down water bottle placed inside to make it watertight.

↑ ANTIQUE VASE
Glass vase with a small neck to display just a few short-stemmed blooms.

↑ OVAL TROUGH
Painted terracotta pot for low floral foam displays.

POTTERY JUG ↑
Ideal for a few flowers with their stems cut short.

TEA LIGHT HOLDER →
Useful for multiple small, informal displays.

CUP AND SAUCER →
Porcelain teacups can hold single flowers.

FLOWER SHAPES

The enormously diverse varieties of flower we see around us can be classified into a limited range of flower shapes. Recognizing the most basic of these shapes is extremely helpful in understanding which types of flowers you should select and how they work best in particular arrangements. Another way to understand this is that there are no "wrong" flowers, but there is a wrong and a right way to use them. The eight flower shapes we have selected here are those that we think are among the most attractive and useful for flower arranging.

FLAT-TOPPED (trachelium) →
Most flat-topped flowers are quite large, but the many tiny flowers arranged in clusters on short stalks that form these flower heads make them look airy and delicate in appearance.
Good for This flower shape is useful for hand-tied bouquets, as it helps to form the required dome shape. It also provides textural interest and detail in both large and small designs.
Flowers Trachelium, Queen Anne's lace, dill

SPEAR →
(delphinium)
Clusters of small flowers on short stalks growing at the top of a stem form a typical spear flower shape. With so many individual flowers on one stem, these flowers are full of colour and interest.
Good for Flowers with elongated stems, such as molucella and delphiniums, provide structure, form, and necessary height in large vases or structural designs.
Flowers Delphiniums, molucella, orchids, gentiana, liatris, lupins, foxgloves, lilacs, Solomon's seal

DOME (hydrangea) →
Large and small domed flowers are real "feature" flowers that provide substance and focus in an arrangement. The flower heads are usually quite dense and provide a strong injection of colour in a design.
Good for This flower shape is suitable for large displays and minimalist designs.
Flowers Hydrangeas, most celosias, chrysanthemums

← REGULAR
(gerbera)
Flowers with the same-shaped petals in a simple circular shape around its centre have what is called radial symmetry: whichever way you divide a regular flower, it has two or three similar parts.
Good for These flowers are adaptable: they can be used on their own in striking designs or as a repeat pattern in a larger arrangement.
Flowers Gerberas, sunflowers, marguerites, daffodils, narcissi, anemones

← GLOBE (allium)
The perfectly round shape of globe flowers means they look most impressive *en masse*, and usually work best in a minimalist design of just one or two types of flower.
Good for These flowers work well in modern and sculptural designs, especially if the strong, straight stems of flowers such as alliums are left as long as possible.
Flowers Alliums, tulips, protea

ROSETTE (rose) ↓
The geometric rosette shape of some flowers makes them ideal for large and small arrangements alike.
Good for These flowers attract the eye easily and so can be used as feature flowers in a mixed display or on their own in a minimalist design.
Flowers Single roses, globe artichokes, ranunculas, peonies, dahlias, carnations

SPRAY (eryngium) →
With their branching stems and large quantity of flower heads, spray flowers are adaptable, and are ideal for mixed arrangements.
Good for If the flower heads are left on their single main stem, they can be used to reinforce the fan shape of a vase display, or provide a mass of colour and interest in hand-tied bouquets. They can also be cut down to provide numerous shorter-stemmed flowers in floral foam designs.
Flowers Eryngium, lilies, spray roses, lisianthus, astrantia

← SPIRE (veronica)
A spire shape has small, stalkless flowers at the tip of a long stem. The flowers open in sequence, usually from the bottom, which helps to create its tapering shape.
Good for These shapes contrast well with softer-petalled flowers, and are useful for breaking the smooth outlines of a domed bouquet or floral foam design.
Flowers Veronica, stocks, antirrhinums, grape hyacinths, hyacinths, lily of the valley, lavender

FOLIAGE TYPES

The aim of using foliage in an arrangement is to provide texture, extra colour, shape, and proportion: whether you design a front-facing arrangement or a three-dimensional display, foliage will help to give it the necessary height, width, depth, and interest that it needs in order to look balanced and substantial. Some foliage works better in large arrangements to fill out and shape the design, while sculptural grasses create interest and height. Other – usually all-year – foliage works better in small designs to give added detail and colour. Ultimately, however, the foliage that you choose for an arrangement will always depend on its seasonal or all-year availability.

ALL-YEAR FOLIAGE

With the exception of ruscus, all-year foliage tends to be short and so is best used for medium-sized and compact arrangements. Choose foliage such as pittosporum, salal gaultheria, eucalyptus, bear grass, snake grass, leather leaf, and black tie and green tie leaves.

← RUSCUS
These attractive feathery leaves on long curved stems add a delicate texture to a design.

← SALAL
This foliage is a dense filler best used for small designs and bouquets.

EUCALYPTUS →
The unusual silver-green leaves, pleasant scent, and handsome arching stems of eucalyptus enhance the shape of a design and add an extra flourish.

SEASONAL FOLIAGE

The tall, straight stems of cotinus, forsythia, privet, red robin, white leaf, and rhododendron are ideal for large displays, and any side shoots can be used at the edges of a design, or in a compact arrangement. Hebe, berried ivy, senecio, hypericum, and alchemilla are best-suited for compact arrangements. Condition seasonal foliage well, or it will quickly droop.

← PRIVET
Tall and dramatic, privet provides an effective backdrop for long-stemmed flowers.

← ALCHEMILLA
With its unusual lime-green colour and lacy appearance, alchemilla is ideal for breaking up a dense mass of flowers. It is pretty enough to be used like a flower in some designs.

RED ROBIN →
This red-stemmed foliage adds a rich colour accent to an autumn display.

EQUIPMENT

There are certain tools and a limited amount of equipment that you need to condition flowers, arrange them properly, and maintain them. This is the essential kit you need to make all the arrangements in this book. Work in a cool room, sweep up leaves and stems from the floor as you work so you don't slip on them, and use a large bucket to condition the flowers and foliage.

STICKY TAPE ↓
Use to bind split stems, make grids across vase tops, and wrap bouquets.

HAND MISTER ↓
Use to refresh or revive blooms with a fine mist of water.

STERILIZING TABLETS →
Add to a vase or container of water to kill bacteria and help to keep the water clear.

FLORIST'S TAPE ↑
Use to bind floral foam to a plastic tray or bowl.

STEM TAPE ↑
Use to cover and seal individually wired flower and foliage stems.

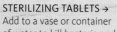

PEARL PINS ↓
For buttonholes and pinning ribbons in place.

PIN CUSHION ↑
Necessary for arranging stems at precise angles.

← POSY BOWL
Shallow plastic bowl designed to hold enough floral foam for a small arrangement.

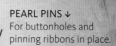

PAINTBRUSH ↓
For dusting any pollen off flower petals.

GREEN TACK →
Useful for attaching fabric and coverings to containers.

PHIAL ↑
For keeping single-stemmed flowers fresh before being presented.

BOTTLE BRUSH ↘
For cleaning vases and containers.

← DEEP BOWL
Plastic bowl that holds enough floral foam for a large front-facing display.

22 GAUGE WIRE ↑
Suitable for wiring larger flower stems, ribbons, and other equipment.

ROSE WIRES ↑
Use for wiring smaller-stemmed flowers and buttonholes.

LONG-STEMMED PHIAL ↑
Attach to short-stemmed flowers in mixed designs.

GARDEN CANES IN VARIOUS SIZES ↓
Useful for providing support and placing ingredients in position.

ELASTIC BANDS ↓
Useful for making up bunches of finer foliage such as bear grass.

RAFFIA ↑
Ideal for binding hand-tied bouquets and arranged stems.

GARDEN STRING ↑
A suitable alternative to raffia.

PLASTIC BOTTLE ↓
Cut-down plastic bottle to hold flowers in water in non-watertight containers.

↑ DECORATIVE COLOURED REEL WIRES
Wires in various colours and thicknesses to bind the stems of flowers or add decorative details.

CHICKEN WIRE ↑
Mould to fit and place in an opaque vase or container to hold the stems of an arrangement in place.

FLORIST'S SCISSORS ↓
Ideal for conditioning and trimming flowers and thin-stemmed foliage.

FLORAL FOAM BLOCK AND TRAY →
Use for medium-sized floral foam arrangements.

CRAFT KNIFE →
Use to condition flowers and cut and trim soaked blocks of floral foam.

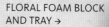

SECATEURS →
Use to trim and split woody-stemmed foliage and thick-stemmed flowers.

CHOOSING AND PREPARING

Select the best-quality flowers available from your local florist or grower, and stay as seasonal as possible with your choices. Depending on the occasion, choose blooms that are still in bud or already beginning to open, and as a general rule, buy a maximum of four to five types of flower in three or four harmonious, or two complementary, colours. If scent is important, ask your florist for advice before you buy and check if the flowers have a light or a stronger, heady scent – it may have an impact on where you intend to place the flowers, as some scents can be overpowering in small rooms.

WHEN TO BUY FLOWERS

For arrangements that will last longer at home, buy flowers such as lilies, amaryllis, roses, ranunculas, and tulips while they are still in bud. However, if you need flowers as a short-term effect for a special occasion such as a wedding, buy flowers that are already beginning to open up so they will look their best on the day.

HEALTHY ROSES

To check whether the roses you want to buy are really fresh and will last well in an arrangement, gently squeeze a few of the flower heads near the base where the petals meet the sepals. If the roses are firm, rather than spongy and soft, they are a better choice and will have a longer life span.

Choose flowers such as lilies with their buds in various stages of opening; they shouldn't all be completely closed and neither should they all be almost open.

An older rose has a soft base and tired-looking petals.

A fresh rose has a firm base and tighter, crisp-looking petals.

INSIDER TIPS

• Remove pollen from flowers such as lilies (see right) to prevent stains on petals or clothing, and prevent allergy sufferers from experiencing any symptoms. Lily pollen is poisonous to cats and dogs so remove it if you own one.

• If you use a clear glass vase, drop a sterilizing tablet into the water and let it dissolve before adding the flowers. The tablet will keep the water clear and help to kill any bacteria.

• To encourage buds to open, take off more leaves. With fewer leaves on the stems, more water and nutrients pass to the flower head. To encourage lilies to open, put the stems in warm water, let the water cool, and repeat.

REMOVING POLLEN
Gently pull the pollen-laden stamens from the centre of the flower with your thumb and forefinger. If you miss a flower and the stamens become powdery, pinch the stamens out in the same way and dust off any stray pollen with a paintbrush.

CONDITIONING

It's important to condition your flowers and foliage as soon as you have bought them so that they remain in peak condition for as long as possible. Strip the excess leaves from the stems (below left) and split the ends of any woody stems (below right). Place all the flower and foliage stems in a bucket of deep cold water for a long drink for about an hour before you start to trim the stems and arrange the flowers – this will help to hydrate the flowers and ensure that they will bloom while they are still fresh. If the flowers have enough to drink at this stage, they shouldn't need quite so much water once they have been arranged in a display.

STRIPPING STEMS

2 Leave a few leaves near the top of each stem, but remove any leaves that might stand in water. Foliage often has shorter stems than flowers, so cut off lower side shoots to create longer stems.

1 Lay the flowers and foliage out on a table. Take one stem, stand it upright on a table, and run a craft knife down the sides of the stem to remove any thorns and unwanted leaves.

SPLITTING STEMS

2 Split the ends of woody stems such as roses, lilac, and cultivated guelder with florist's scissors. This increases the surface area of the plant cells in these thicker foliage and flower stems so they take in more water.

1 Make a diagonal cut about 2.5cm (1in) from the base of each stem to encourage the stems to take up more water and hydrate the flower heads.

MAINTENANCE

To prolong the life and look of your flowers, change the water – or mist floral foam displays and moisten the foam – every other day. If you use flower food, change the water every four or five days. Stems in vase arrangements also need to be re-cut every few days, as their ends soon become waterlogged and mushy, restricting the flow of water up to the flower and causing the flowers to droop and lose their petals more quickly. Re-cutting each stem re-hydrates the flower heads and keeps them looking fresh. There are also other ways to revive particular flowers and neaten split stems if your display begins to look a little tired.

MISTING

If it is a hot day when you prepare and condition your flowers, use a hand spray filled with water to refresh or revive them. Mist the flower heads from a distance of 20cm (8in) or so; don't get too close, or you may drench the petals and spoil them. Flowers such as hydrangeas particularly benefit from misting. A hand spray is also vital for misting floral foam arrangements, bouquets, and buttonholes, as the stems will be out of water for a long period.

RE-CUTTING STEMS

Trim the stems with an angled cut 2.5–5cm (1–2in) at the end, depending on how long your stems are to begin with. If the flowers and foliage have woody stems, re-split the stems after you have trimmed them (p27). Then change the water and replace the flowers. If you have used an opaque vase, you can maintain the height of the original arrangement by packing a piece of cellophane or something similar into the base of the vase before you replace the flowers.

Trim all the stems by cutting them at an angle with florist's scissors.

INSIDER TIPS

• Bacteria can build up in water-filled vases, particularly in the corners, which can kill the flowers. Clean your vases thoroughly after each use with hot water, washing-up liquid, and a bottle brush to scrub the edges of the vase well.

• **Keep arrangements** out of direct sunlight and away from radiators to prolong their life.

• If moss discolours, put it in a sink and pour a kettle of boiling water over it to revive it.

CLEANING A VASE
Use a bottle brush to clean your vases and containers thoroughly every time you finish using them. This type of brush can be angled easily into awkward corners to lift out dirt and bacteria.

REVIVING FLOWERS

Lay floppy amaryllis or delphiniums on a table, prop up the stem ends so they tilt upwards, fill the stems with water and leave for an hour or so until the stems are more rigid. The wilting petals of hydrangea are tough enough to survive being submerged in water for a minimum of two hours, or overnight, to revive them. To straighten and strengthen floppy gerberas, trim the stems, wrap them in newspaper, and leave in a vase of water for a few hours.

SPLIT STEMS

The fleshy stems of flowers such as amaryllis, hyacinths, and calla lilies can begin to look unsightly in a clear glass vase or container of water if they split. To prevent this happening, wrap a length of clear sticky tape two or three times around the base of each stem after you have conditioned the flowers. This will ensure that the stems remain neat and won't splay. Then place the flower stems in the arrangement as usual.

Wrap gerbera stems in newspaper up to their necks, stand in a vase of water, and allow the newspaper to soak up the water and draw it up the lengths of the stems.

Gerberas absorb water both through the base of the stem and by osmosis through the surface area of the stem along its length.

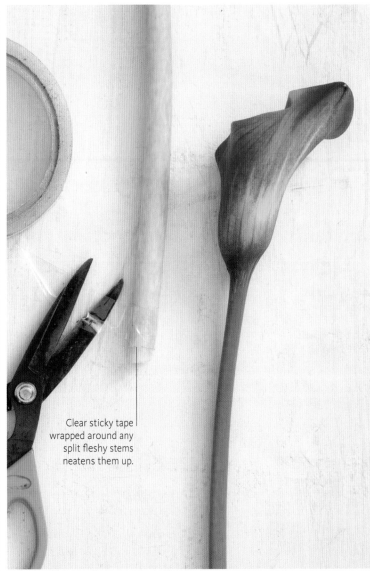

Clear sticky tape wrapped around any split fleshy stems neatens them up.

FRONT-FACING VASE ARRANGEMENT

This step-by-step sequence explains how to arrange a vase of flowers in a simple but effective front-facing design. These straightforward steps will equip you with all the essential knowledge and skills you need to create any vase arrangement.

Before you arrange your flowers and foliage, cut the stems at an angle (keeping all the stems as long as possible until you arrange them), split any woody stems, take the pollen out of lilies, if using, and give them all a long drink in deep water (p27).

Basic materials

Flared vase
Sterilizing tablet (if using a clear glass vase)
Chicken wire (optional if using an opaque vase)
Florist's scissors

1 Fill a clean, well-washed, flared vase with fresh water and, if you are using a clear glass vase, add a sterilizing tablet. Arrange all the flowers and foliage into separate piles. Ideally, you want to have 5–8 stems each of two different types of foliage and 3–5 stems each of four different types of flower.

↓ eucalyptus and ruscus stems

↓ dark pink antirrhinums

↓ pink lilies

↓ pink lisianthus

↓ pink single roses

2 Place 3–4 stems of one type of foliage in the vase. These stems will naturally fall at an angle against the sides of the vase, creating a loose fan shape, and form a basic framework. They are designed to be slightly shorter than the other foliage. If you use an opaque vase, insert chicken wire into the vase first to ensure that each stem rests at the correct angle (right).

3 Add the second type of foliage in between the first stems. Stand each stem in front of the vase first to compare it to the display and gauge how much to trim it. Then cut and split it again and add it to the arrangement at an angle. If it still looks too tall, re-cut it and arrange it again. Shorter stems of foliage should stand at the front of the vase, with longer stems at the back and sides.

4 Once you have built up a good basic, but still quite sparse, fan shape, stop adding any more foliage for now.

5 Add the first variety of flower – usually those with the largest flower heads. Hold each flower stem at an angle in front of the vase where you think you would like to place it, then trim the end of the stem and insert it at an angle. At least one of these stems should be taller than the rest and stand at the back of the arrangement; stems placed at the front of the vase should be shortest.

6 Add the next variety of flower, angling each stem in front of the vase first to check its placing and height, and then inserting it at an angle. Although you need to judge the length of each stem individually, the aim is to create a graduated shape that is low at the front and tall at the back.

7 Turn the vase around so that you can view the display from the side and check on its graduated shape. If you use a clear vase, it's also worth glancing at the stems inside the vase at this point to check that they are positioned at an angle, which shows that you are building up the design in the correct way.

8 Add the third variety of flower, checking the height and position of each flower before you add it to the design. Place these flowers evenly through the design where there are gaps.

9 Insert the stems of the last type of flower in the same way. Using four varieties of flower in a vase arrangement ensures a rich texture and range of colour, and creates more movement through the arrangement.

10 Add small stems of foliage at the edges and front to hide the top of the vase. As these stems are shorter, ensure that they sit in water; top up the vase if necessary once you have positioned it. Change the water every few days and re-cut the stems (if you have used chicken wire, lift the whole arrangement, with the chicken wire intact, out of the vase, trim the stems, and replace it in fresh water).

HAND-TIED BOUQUET

Our aim when making up a hand-tied bouquet is to keep the look of the bouquet quite compact, develop a rounded, or domed, shape with the flowers and foliage, and create a spiral effect with the stems. These are all aesthetic details that define our signature style.

Arranging a hand-tied bouquet is a methodical process. If you add your groups of flowers in the same sequence and turn the bunch slightly in the same direction every time you add a flower or a foliage stem, you should ensure that you won't place the same flowers next to each other as the bunch builds up. The binding point governs the size of a bouquet: if you hold the stems lower down, the arrangement will be looser, and the stems longer. A slightly higher binding point – holding the bunch of flowers about halfway to two-thirds of the way up their stems – will create the compact bouquet we prefer.

Basic materials

Florist's scissors
Raffia or garden string

1 Choose 3–6 stems each of five different flower varieties and 15 stems of foliage such as salal, and then condition them (p27).

← pink celosias

↓ astrantia

↓ pale pink single roses

↓ dark pink calla lilies

mauve → tracheliums

2 Arrange the flowers into individual piles so you can clearly see the colours and sizes of the different flower heads.

3 Choose a focal flower for the centre of the bouquet. It should be something that is fairly big. In this case, a pink rose is a perfect choice. Add 3–4 stems of foliage in a circle around this first flower. The flower should sit just beneath the tips of the leaves. Hold the bunch at the binding point with your left hand if you are right-handed, and vice-versa if you are left-handed.

4 Pick another variety of flower and insert it into the bunch at the point where your thumb rests. Insert the stem at an angle so the end of the stem points towards your body and the flower head is angled away from you.

5 Place one of each of the other flowers around the foliage, turning the bunch slightly in the same direction after you have added each bloom. The flowers should, like the first rose, sit slightly lower than the tips of the foliage leaves.

6 Roughly trim the longer stems if the bunch becomes top-heavy. Don't cut the stems too short; you will need to trim all the stems properly later on. Add another circle of foliage at an angle, turning the bunch slightly as you work. The spiral of stems should now be apparent.

7 Look at the top of the bunch to check the position of the flowers and the balance of colours. Arrange the next sequence of flowers slightly lower around the sides to begin forming the domed shape. Use up the remaining flowers and foliage, angling these stems so that they sit even lower around the edges of the bunch.

8 Wrap a length of raffia or garden string a few times around the top of the binding point – immediately above your hand – and tie the ends firmly in a knot to secure the bunch. Trim off any excess raffia.

9 Trim the ends of the stems straight across so that the bunch can stand upright in a vase and all the stems will be in water. Re-split any woody stems.

10 A well-arranged, securely-tied bouquet like this should be able to stand upright unaided, as the spiral stems give it stability. Place the bouquet in a vase or, if it is a gift for someone, keep it in fresh, cool water until you are ready to wrap it and tie it with a ribbon (pp46–49), and then present it.

FLORAL FOAM ARRANGEMENT

A floral foam display is ideal if you want to create a low, compact design or a defined shape on a larger scale. Each flower and foliage stem is inserted at an angle to create the rounded or graduated contour that is so characteristic of these arrangements.

Floral foam must be soaked before you trim it, position it, and then arrange the flowers and foliage. Drop a block of floral foam into a bowl or bucket of water and lift it out as soon as it appears to have completely absorbed water or sunk to the bottom of the bucket; don't leave it in the water or it will begin to disintegrate. It's also worth using a hand spray regularly while you work to refresh the flowers.

Basic materials

Floral foam
Posy bowl
Craft knife
Stem tape
Florist's scissors

1 Use 6–8 stems each of two different types of foliage, 7–11 stems each of three varieties of flower (or 2–3 stems if using spray flowers) for this small arrangement. Condition your flowers and foliage (p27). The stems will be cut quite short when you arrange them, so they don't need to be left too long when you condition them.

↓ purple veronica

white → lisianthus

eucalyptus → stems

↑ salal stems

↑ white single roses

2 Place half a block of soaked floral foam in the posy bowl, trim the corners of the foam with a craft knife, and bind it to the bowl with stem tape.

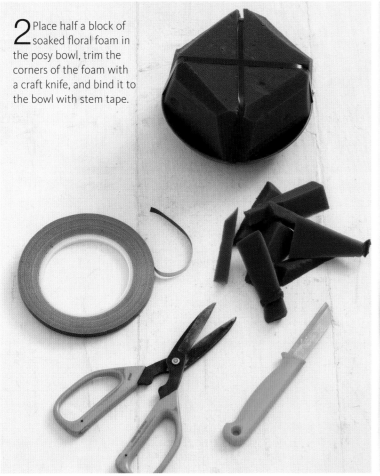

3 Trim the smaller stems from the different sprays of foliage and use one variety of foliage to create a skeleton framework: insert a stem at an angle in each side of the foam at the base (so the leaves are angled downwards to hide the base of the bowl), and three stems in a line across the top of the foam. Press the stems firmly, but not too far, into the foam – about 2cm (¾in) deep.

4 Add a few stems of the second type of foliage at an angle to fill the natural spaces in the foam. You want to achieve an even, rounded shape with the angled leaves, but not all the foam should be hidden at this stage.

5 Use the largest flower heads next: trim each stem to 10cm (4in) or so and insert it at an angle (the flower heads inserted around the base of the foam should be angled downwards, and those at the top angled upwards). Give the flowers and foliage a quick misting.

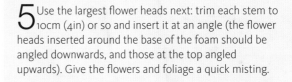

6 Insert the flowers evenly around the arrangement. Move the arrangement round as you work so that you distribute the flowers evenly. Here, four flowers have been inserted around the lower part of the foam, and three around the upper part.

7 Add a smaller flower next; spire-shaped flowers work well in an arrangement like this. Insert them at an angle in between the first flowers. Allow these spiky flowers to rise up out of the arrangement slightly to break the rounded contours of the other blooms.

9 Turn the arrangement round one last time to check for any gaps or visible foam, and fill or cover them with a stem of foliage.

8 If you use a variety of spray-shaped flower, cut off the shorter stems to use as individual blooms. Insert them into any obvious gaps in the arrangement.

10 Give the flowers and foliage a good misting with a hand mister. Before putting the display in position, tilt it over a kitchen sink to allow excess water to drain away, then dry the base of the container (this is especially important if you intend to hang a floral foam display as a pew end, for example). To prolong the life of the flowers, the foam must be kept moist: every 3–4 days, sit the arrangement on the draining board of the kitchen sink and gently pour a jug of water over it. Then mist the flowers and foliage again.

WIRED BUTTONHOLE

The point of wiring a single, beautiful flower in perfect condition is so that the flower head and any leaves surrounding it can be gently manipulated into the perfect angles once the buttonhole has been attached to the lapel of a jacket.

Fine wires and green stem tape are used to replicate the slim, smooth flower stem. The tape also seals in moisture to help the flower stay fresher for a little longer. It's important to keep the lengths of wire as straight as possible to avoid creating a bumpy effect that would look unsightly against the lapel of a suit.

Basic materials

Florist's scissors
Silver rose wires
Stem tape
22 gauge wire
Pearl pin

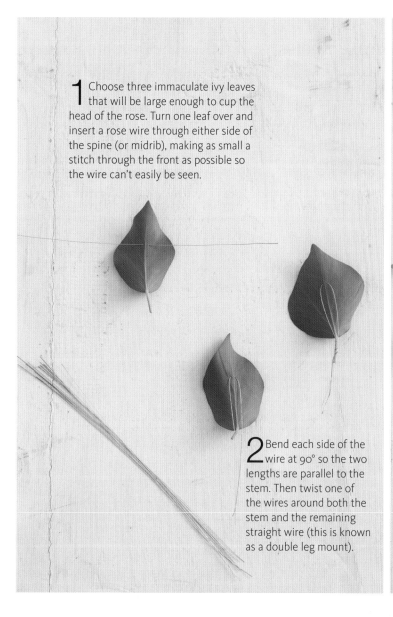

1 Choose three immaculate ivy leaves that will be large enough to cup the head of the rose. Turn one leaf over and insert a rose wire through either side of the spine (or midrib), making as small a stitch through the front as possible so the wire can't easily be seen.

2 Bend each side of the wire at 90° so the two lengths are parallel to the stem. Then twist one of the wires around both the stem and the remaining straight wire (this is known as a double leg mount).

3 Split a long length of stem tape in half with scissors (this is easily done by running the slightly open blades of the scissors up the centre of the length of tape). Using thinner stem tape ensures a finer and more delicate result.

4 Attach one end of the thin stem tape to the top of the leaf stem. Wind the tape around and down the stem and wires, keeping the tape taut and stretching it as you wind it. Wind the tape down to the ends of the wires and back up again slightly. Pull off the excess tape with your fingers and seal it down. Repeat the process with the other two leaves.

5 To prepare the rose, bunch several rose wires together and fold them over the scissor blades at one end to create a small "U" shape in each wire. Snip off these folded ends to make staples. Press these staples into the sepals – the small green leaves immediately below the petals – so they are held in place.

6 Trim the rose stem at an angle to 2.5cm (1in) long and push a 22 gauge wire up through the base of the stem. Then use a thin rose wire to pierce the side of the stem. Push this wire halfway through the stem so you have an equal length of the wire at each side. Bend each side of the rose wire at 90° so the two lengths are parallel to the stem. Twist one of the rose wires around the rose stem, the 22 gauge wire, and the remaining length of rose wire in a double leg mount.

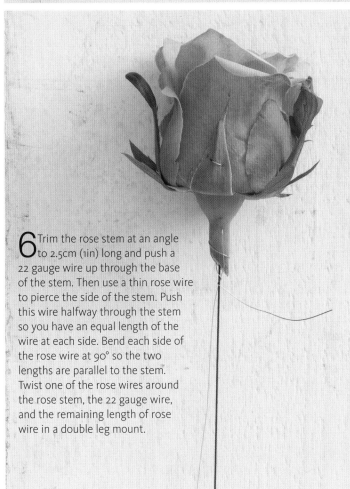

7 Wind another length of thinned stem tape around the stem of the rose and the wires. Wrap the tape down to the ends of the wires and back up again slightly. Pull off the excess tape with your fingers and seal it down cleanly.

8 Place one of the wired leaves against the side of the rose so that the top of the leaf stem aligns with the top of the flower stem. Wrap only the wires together with stem tape so the stems themselves remain separated.

9 Bind the other two leaves to the flower in the same way, ensuring they are evenly spaced. Don't cut the length of florist's tape off when you attach the last leaf; you will need it shortly.

10 Trim the three leaf wires to different lengths to create a graduated effect. This means that as you push them against the 22 gauge wire they align smoothly and don't create a lumpy effect. Then cut the 22 gauge wire down to about 8cm (3in).

11 Wrap the loose end of the stem tape around the trimmed, graduated wires and down around the rose wire. Twist the tape around the base of the 22 gauge wire and then wind it back up the wire a little.

12 Massage the bound stem tape slightly in your fingers to seal it properly and then pull or cut off any excess tape. The wired stems should look and feel like one smooth flower stem.

13 To attach the wired rose to a jacket with a buttonhole, insert the wired stem through the buttonhole, and thread a pin through the underside of the lapel and round the stem to secure the rose in place.

14 Viewed from the front, only the rose and leaves are visible; gently tweak the leaves and flower head to show them off at their best angle.

ALTERNATIVE If a jacket has no buttonhole, place the wired rose against the front of a lapel, insert a pearl pin through the material, over the wired stem, and through the material again to secure the flower.

TYING

If you want to give flowers to someone as a gift, a few professional touches such as tying the arrangement skilfully can make all the difference between a sophisticated hand-tied bouquet and a rather loose, floppy bunch of flowers.

Even if you have bought a simple bunch of flowers, it's still worth unwrapping the bunch, rearranging the blooms, and re-tying them neatly so that they look their best.

The best materials to bind a bouquet are seagrass, raffia, and garden string. If you want to use a ribbon, secure the bunch at the binding point first and then tie the ribbon around the flower stems.

1 Lay the flowers and foliage on a bench or table and arrange them into a loosely spiralled bunch. You can, if you prefer, arrange them as a hand-tied bouquet in your hand (pp34–37).

2 Wrap a long length of seagrass (or raffia or garden string) twice around the stems at the binding point (just above your hand).

3 Bring the two ends of the raffia together and tie them together once. Then repeat the procedure with each end of seagrass to create a reef knot.

4 Pull the reef knot tight so it is secure and then trim the ends of the seagrass and the flower and foliage stems so they look neat.

WRAPPING

It's always best to wrap a hand-tied bouquet before you give it to someone as a gift: the wrapping paper helps to protect delicate petals in transit; and a well-wrapped bouquet makes a much more pleasing present.

Depending on the style, shape, and size of your bouquet and the colours of the flowers, choose a length of tasteful wrapping paper, cellophane, or simple brown paper, and select a ribbon that matches the predominant colour of your bouquet.

1 Fold the wrapping paper in half at a slight angle (you may choose to have the pattern on the inside, as here). Place the bouquet of flowers on top of the paper so the binding point rests on the folded edge of the paper.

2 Fold one half of the wrapping paper carefully over the front of the flowers so the folded edge of the paper aligns with the outer edge of the bouquet.

3 Roll the bouquet up inside the rest of the paper, or fold the other half of the paper over the bouquet – whichever feels easier. Once the flowers are enclosed in the cone shape created by the paper, seal both sides of paper together with a small piece of clear sticky tape.

4 To attach a ribbon around the base of the cone, you may need to pinch the folded paper together slightly first. Then wrap the ribbon twice around the stems and the base of the paper and secure the ends in a large bow. To prevent the bow looking lopsided, take the loops up rather than down as you tie them.

THROUGH THE YEAR

Seasonal flowers and foliage look their best when they are bought or picked in season, and they last longer. These arrangements give you an idea of the wonderful variety of flowers available throughout the year, and how you can use them.

TULIPS IN CUPS

Depending on the occasion or surroundings, the greatest impact can sometimes be made with the simplest of displays. This small, informal collection of plain cups and loosely arranged tulips is perfect for a dressing table, kitchen dresser, as individual place settings, or positioned in a row along a shelf or a table at a children's tea party. Choose tulip colours that suit the surroundings and limit yourself to a maximum of two colours; tulips that are the same colour, or which harmonize or complement each other, make a stronger visual statement. They will last for a week if you keep them in good condition (pp28–29).

HOW TO ARRANGE

1 Clean the cups thoroughly and fill them two-thirds full of water.

2 Loosely arrange four yellow and four orange tulip stems in one hand. Strip off any leaves that might end up sitting in the water and trim the ends of the stems so that the flower heads will sit just above the rim of each cup.

3 Place the stems in a cup and adjust them so that they fall naturally in a random and informal way. The straight sides of the cups will make the tulips easier to arrange. Repeat the same process for the two remaining cup arrangements. Then top up the water to just below the rim of each cup.

INSIDER TIP

• This simple arrangement works best with a minimum of three cups of tulips, but make up as few or as many of these arrangements as you like to suit the space you have available and to create the right effect.

Flowers

← 4 yellow
tulips per cup

← 4 orange
tulips per cup

Other materials

3 straight-sided plain cups
(10 x 7cm/4 x 3in) or any
simply coloured or plain
cups or teacups
Florist's scissors

Possible substitutions

Ranunculas, mixed narcissi,
or daffodils

WHITE CUBE

This tonal composition of creamy white flowers is arranged so that the individual blooms are bunched in four equal groups to create a chequerboard effect. Although this is intended to be a monochrome all-round vase arrangement, its clever design gradually draws your eye to the subtle differences in flower shapes and the hints of green and yellow that intersperse the white tones. Small-headed spray roses make a good substitute if you can't find one of these particular varieties of flower. The arrangement is best placed on a low coffee table so that the flowers can be seen from above, and it should last for a week if you keep the flowers in good condition (pp28–29).

HOW TO ARRANGE

1 Gather each variety of flower into a hand-tied bunch with the stems straight rather than spiralled: take two stems and add more flowers at an upright angle to them, turning the bunch around slightly in the same direction in your hand as you add to it. Each bunch must be roughly the same size, so use fewer hyacinth stems than you would narcissi, for example.

2 Tie each bunch at the binding point with a length of raffia.

3 Trim the stems of all the flowers to the same length.

4 Fill two-thirds of the vase with water and arrange the bunches of flowers so that they stand upright in the vase and overhang the edges slightly. There should be no gaps between the separate "squares" of flowers. Finally, top up the vase with water.

INSIDER TIPS

• This design can be recreated in any size; the smaller the container, the fewer flowers you will need, though use a minimum of five stems of each flower to achieve the same look.

• You may need to re-cut the tulip stems more often than the other flowers, as they will continue to grow after they have been arranged.

Flowers

30 paper →
white narcissi

↓ 25 white
ranunculas

25 white
single tulips ↓

↓ 15 white
hyacinths

Other materials

White cube vase (18 x 18cm/7 x 7in)
Raffia
Florist's scissors

Possible substitutions

For a yellow design use: daffodils (for narcissi); yellow freesias (for tulips); yellow single roses (for hyacinths); yellow spray roses (for ranunculas)

VIBRANT BOUQUET

This hand-tied bouquet of colourful flowers is made up of contrasting blues and oranges that enhance each other so that the blooms sing with intensity. If you use hyacinths and grape hyacinths from your garden, cut the stems as long as possible; if they are much shorter than the other stems, reduce the number of flowers and cut their stems shorter to make a posy. If grape hyacinths are hard to find, try using lilac freesia instead. This bouquet looks sensational in an orange or black glass vase as a table centrepiece, or it could make a gorgeous gift for a birthday or for Mother's Day. It should last at least a week.

HOW TO ARRANGE

1 Divide the different flower varieties into separate piles. Hold a hyacinth in your hand at the binding point. This bouquet is compact, so keep the binding point just higher than halfway up the stem. Add another flower at an angle, twisting the bunch around slightly in one direction in your hand as you do so.

2 Add a stem of salal and one of each of the flower varieties (add the grape hyacinths in groups of three for a better effect). Recess the tulips slightly, as they will continue to grow. Check that you are happy with the arrangement, then add more stems at the same angle to create a spiral stem effect. Keep turning the bunch around slightly in the same direction as you work.

3 Arrange the last layer of flowers a little lower around the edges to give a slightly domed look.

4 Tie the bunch at the binding point with a length of raffia or garden string and secure in a knot.

5 Cut the stems at an angle so they are roughly the same length and will all be able to sit in water. If you are giving the bouquet as a gift, stand it in fresh water until you need it, then wrap it in paper and tie it with a ribbon (pp48–49) to present it.

Flowers and foliage

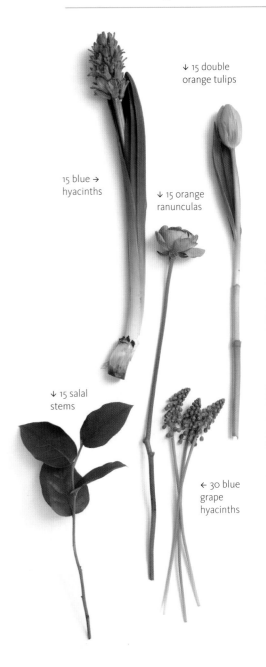

↓ 15 double orange tulips

15 blue → hyacinths

↓ 15 orange ranunculas

↓ 15 salal stems

← 30 blue grape hyacinths

Other materials

Florist's scissors
Raffia or garden string

Possible substitutions

Lilac freesias (for grape hyacinths); ruscus or variegated pittosporum (for salal)

ROMANTIC WEDDING

With their cheerful, uplifting colours that carry the promise of bright days ahead, yellow flowers are perfect for these classic, yet quite informal, wedding designs. Condition them really well before arranging them (pp26–27), and keep them misted or in water until the last minute (and dry the bouquet stems with a cloth so they don't spoil the bride's dress).

BUTTONHOLE

7 lily of the valley
3 lily of the valley leaves

BOUQUET

10 yellow freesias
10 cultivated guelder
7 cream spray roses
10 cream parrot tulips

← lily of the valley

← cultivated guelder

← yellow freesias

cream → spray roses

← cream tulips

← yellow tulips

cream → parrot tulips

← flat moss

BUTTONHOLE

Sweetly scented, delicate lily of the valley flowers make an unusual but attractive choice for a buttonhole. This arrangement is simple to create, as the flower stems don't need to be wired.

1 Give the flowers a good drink of water the day before, then trim off any leaves and simply gather seven stems of lily of the valley together in a mini spiral of flowers.

2 Add a couple of the leaves around the back of the buttonhole, and fold a third leaf in half and place it at the front of the arrangement.

3 Secure the buttonhole with a length of raffia tied in a neat knot and supply it with a pearl-tipped pin to attach it onto the lapel of a jacket.

BOUQUET

This gorgeous cream, yellow, and green bouquet needs to be slightly more rounded and domed than a normal hand-tied bouquet.

1 Divide the different flowers into separate piles. Hold a flower stem in your hand and add another variety of flower to it. Twist the bunch around slightly in your hand as you do so.

2 Add more stems at the same angle to create a spiral stem effect. Keep turning the bunch in the same direction as you work. Add one of each of the different flowers until you have included all the blooms and have a balanced look. Recess the tulips slightly if you make the bouquet the day before it is needed.

3 Arrange the last two layers of flowers slightly lower around the edges for a domed effect.

4 Tie the bunch with a length of raffia or string. Cover the raffia with a long length of thick cream ribbon, wrapped several times around the stems, and tied in a knot. Trim the stem ends straight across with secateurs.

ROSE TOPIARY TREE

The restrained elegance of this spray rose floral foam arrangement is due in large part to its limited ingredients – this is another example of a mass of just one variety of flower creating an eye-catching display. The proportions of the arrangement are designed so that the container is slightly taller than the twigs, and the twigs are a little longer than the rose ball. Floral foam balls are sold in various sizes, and although this display has been made with the smallest-sized foam ball available, it can be recreated on a much larger scale. This handsome design would look good on a desk in a study or a library, a hall table, or on a side table in a living room. It needs misting every other day to keep the blooms fresh, and should last four to five days.

HOW TO ARRANGE

1 Tie the bundle of birch twigs securely with a length of raffia about 10–12cm (4–5in) up from the base of the bundle. Tie the ends of the twigs with another length of raffia. Cut the branched tips of the birch twigs off just above the top raffia tie.

Flowers and foliage

← 1 bundle of birch twigs

← 15 'Mimi Eden' spray roses open and in bud

↓ moss

Other materials

Opaque urn (20cm/8in high)
Raffia
Florist's scissors
Cellophane
1 block floral foam
1 small floral foam ball

Possible substitutions

Spray carnations (for spray roses); bamboo (for birch twigs)

2 Line the urn with a square of cellophane if it is not watertight. Place a soaked square of floral foam, cut to fit, inside the urn.

3 Push the soaked foam ball onto the tied twigs, then push the base of the twigs into the square foam in the urn. Cut off the top raffia binding under the foam ball, but keep the lower binding in place.

4 Trim the stems of the buds and roses to 5cm (2in). Group two or three rose heads together and press them into the foam ball. Fill in the gaps around them with buds. Continue until the ball is covered.

INSIDER TIP

• If you like the idea of converting the rose ball into a hanging display (like a pomander), push a length of wire through the centre of the ball after you've soaked it, wrap one end of the wire around a small, short twig to hold the wire securely in place, and fashion the other end into a loop to hang the ball up. Cover the ball in roses or peonies and hang it from an overhanging branch near or above a table set for lunch in the garden.

• Moss should last well in an arrangement like this, particularly if you mist it with water when you spray the roses. If the moss begins to discolour, place it in a bowl, pour boiling water over it to revive it, and rearrange it over the floral foam.

5 Trim the cellophane so that it is level with the rim of the urn, then cover the square foam and cellophane with moss so that they are both hidden.

HYDRANGEA BALL

Minimal ingredients create maximum impact with this simple vase arrangement. The aim is to work with a limited palette of colours and flowers, and not to fill the bowl up to the rim with petals. Hydrangeas are ideal for this design, as they are one of the few flowers whose petals are coarse enough to tolerate sitting in water; most are too thin and delicate, and soon turn slimy. It's worth trying to find something similar to this twisted, woven ring of dried vine around the base of the bowl, as it brings added interest and another natural element to the display. This design looks good on a coffee table or in a modern bathroom and will last for a week if you refresh the water and re-cut the stems.

HOW TO ARRANGE

1 Pour a small amount of water into the fish bowl – the water should only be about 5cm (2in) deep.

2 Cut the stems of three of the flower heads slightly shorter and arrange them first, placing the ends of the stems in the water.

3 Take the remaining three flower heads and carefully insert their slightly longer stems in between the bottom layer of flowers until the stems sit in the water. The lower layer of flower heads should help to keep these uppermost blooms stable in this all-round display. Fluff out the hydrangea petals so they are not squashed.

Flowers

↓ 6 pink hydrangea flower heads

A NATURAL BASE
A ring of twisted vine adds texture and interest to this flower arrangement.

Other materials

Fish bowl (41cm/16in high)
Florist's scissors
Woven vine base or similar

Possible substitution

Gypsophila

SUNFLOWER VASE

The loosely arranged sunflowers in this rustic, hessian-covered column vase are massed to give a sense of organic growth – almost as if they are still growing in a field – and together they create a strong, textural look. This modern design is all about using your own visual judgement to create a basic domed shape with added height and shorter flowers that hide any unsightly stems from view. It should last for ten days.

HOW TO ARRANGE

1 Place the hessian fabric on a table and lay the vase on its side on the fabric. Fold the fabric around the vase, then secure a double length of seagrass around the vase and tie it in a knot. Stand the vase upright, rearrange the hessian folds, and bind them against the sides of the vase with as many diagonal double lengths of seagrass as you think you need.

2 Half-fill the vase with water. Strip all the leaves from the sunflower stems so the flower heads don't droop.

3 Hold a sunflower in one hand and add a few blooms to it, twisting the stems around slightly in one direction in your hand as you do so to create a rough spiral effect. Add a few more stems, then trim them to approximately the same length. Instead of tying the stems together at this point, drop them straight into the vase. This loose spiral arrangement provides a criss-cross framework to support the remaining stems.

4 Add some taller stems at the back and shorter stems at the front and sides to hide the neck of the vase and any visible stems. Aim to achieve an organic, not tight, look. Nip off any extra leaves beneath the flower heads. Then top up the vase almost to the rim with water.

Flowers

← 11 giant sunflowers

↓ 9 'Teddy Bear' sunflowers

← 9 black sunflowers

Other materials

Column vase (41cm/16in high)
Hessian fabric or sacking material
   (approx 1.2m x 50cm/4ft x 20in)
Seagrass cord
Florist's scissors

Possible substitutions

Large-headed chrysanthemums
   (for all sunflower varieties)

FIESTA BOUQUET

This spiral hand-tied bouquet emphasizes the rich colours and textures of the different flowers and foliage. Celosia flower heads are heavy and easier to use in a compact bouquet where they are supported by other blooms, so use quite a high binding point to arrange these flowers and foliage. If you can't find cotinus, the bouquet will still look striking with any variety of green foliage. Give it away as a gift, or put it in a rustic container and place it at the centre of a table set for Sunday lunch. It will last for at least seven days if you keep the flowers in good condition (pp28–29).

HOW TO ARRANGE

1 Sort the flowers and foliage into individual piles. Hold the stem of one flower, such as a celosia, in your hand at the binding point and arrange three to four stems of salal around it. Add another variety of flower at an angle, twisting the stems around slightly in one direction in your hand.

2 Add one of each of all the flowers and foliage at the same angle to create a spiral stem effect, turning the arrangement in the same direction as you do so. Look at the top of the bouquet to check that you like the arrangement of blooms, then add the remaining stems. Cut the stems down a little if they are becoming hard to handle. Arrange the last two layers of flowers and foliage a little lower around the edges to create a slightly domed effect. Add a few stems of salal around the edges of the bouquet to frame the flowers.

3 Tie the arrangement with raffia or garden string secured in a knot.

4 Cut the stems straight across with a pair of secateurs so that they are all the same length. If the bouquet is a gift, keep the stems in water until you give it away.

INSIDER TIP

• Cotinus is long-stemmed; the lower half has bigger leaves while the upper part bears small leaves, and both create good texture. It's a shame to waste the lower part, so cut the stems in half and use both parts in arrangements.

Flowers and foliage

7 alstroemeria ↓

↓ 7 orange spray roses

↓ 5 protea

↓ 6 hypericum berry stems

6 cotinus stems↓

↑ 5 red celosia

← 6 salal stems

Other materials

Florist's scissors
Raffia or garden string
Secateurs

Possible substitutions

Trachelium (for celosia); roses (for protea); freesias (for spray roses); eryngium (for alstroemeria)

ORANGE FISH BOWL

The iridescent colour of the fish bowl in this contemporary all-round vase arrangement sets the tone for the eclectic mix of flowers and foliage that rest on top of it. It is designed to be compact yet quite loose and unstructured to create a contrast with the very smooth, uniform curves of the bowl; chicken wire placed inside the bowl helps to keep the stems at the right angle. This design will provide a bright injection of colour in a modern kitchen, bathroom, conservatory, or office boardroom and should last for at least a week if you keep the flowers in good condition (pp28–29).

HOW TO ARRANGE

1 Place the chicken wire inside the bowl and half-fill the bowl with water.

2 Cut down the long stems of cotinus and use a few of the shorter stems to create a basic framework.

3 Add a few dahlias around the edge of the bowl, then add a second layer of dahlias so they appear to almost rest on the lower layer. Add a few more stems of cotinus to break up the blooms if they look too dense.

4 Add the gloriosa lilies, placing them evenly around the arrangement. Their elongated petals add an elegant contrast to the round puff-ball effect of the dahlias, so the lilies should sit slightly higher than the other blooms. Then fill the bowl to the top with more water.

Flowers and foliage

← 5 stems cotinus

← 5 orange dahlias

7 gloriosa lilies ↑ with short stems

← 5 yellow dahlias

Other materials

Orange fish bowl (20cm/8in high)
Chicken wire
Florist's scissors

Possible substitutions

Sunflowers and celosia (for dahlias); upright amaranthus (for gloriosa lilies); lilies (for cotinus)

JEWEL DAHLIAS

This mass of dahlias is designed to create a sensational impact: their intricate petal formations and intense colours shine like jewels in an old jewellery box, while the mix of buds, semi-open, and fully open blooms add interest and texture. Whether you gather dahlias from the garden or buy them, ensure their strong colours mix harmoniously together and don't clash. This display will look lovely on a chest of drawers, a traditional writing desk, or a hall table, and should last for a week or more.

HOW TO ARRANGE

1 Line the inside of the box with cellophane or a similar material. Cut the tops off four water bottles (or more or less, depending on how large your box is) and arrange them so they fill the box. Arrange chicken wire in the two rear bottles for the taller flowers, then half-fill all the bottles with water.

2 Arrange some stems at the back first: trim the stems so the flower heads cluster together just below the edge of the box lid, and arrange them in the bottles so they rest against the opened lid. Use the chicken wire to guide their angle and position. Place about five stems in each bottle.

3 Cut the stems slightly shorter as you fill up the front of the bottles at the back, and shorter still for the bottles at the front, to create a graduated effect. Arrange some shorter-stemmed flowers at the sides, too, to create an even effect. Put the wooden box in position and top up the bottles with water.

SIMPLE EQUIPMENT
Use cellophane to catch any drips and protect the lining of the box, and chicken wire inside the bottles to provide effective support for the flowers.

Flowers

↓ 5 'Black Fox' dahlias

↓ 5 'Boy Scout' dahlias

5 'Red Fox' dahlias ↓

↓ 5 'Stratus' dahlias

5 'Red Cap' dahlias →

Other materials

Old wooden box or similar (approx 30 x 20cm/12 x 8in)
Cellophane
4 large plastic water bottles
Chicken wire
Florist's scissors

Possible substitutions

Large and small sunflowers, big-bloomed chrysanthemums, hydrangeas

TABLE CENTREPIECE

This informal basket centrepiece has a watertight container tucked snugly inside it that acts like a vase, while chicken wire inside the rim of the container ensures that all the stems are angled in the right direction. It's important to keep all the stems short in this arrangement so that the proportions of the flowers and foliage match the size and shape of the basket.

1 Place a watertight container inside a 12in (30cm) round wicker basket. Arrange the chicken wire inside the container and fill the container with water. Create a skeleton framework of foliage with short stems of ivy. These stems should be angled so that their leaves fall softly over the sides of the bowl.

2 Add short stems of cotinus to give even coverage through the framework without it being overfull.

3 Add the roses next, as they are the biggest flower heads. Arrange them evenly through the arrangement.

4 Add the blackberries and hypericum and then the sunflowers to finish.

MIXED EXOTIC ARRANGEMENT

This crisp white and green vase arrangement, with its green berries, is warmed up gently by exotic cymbidium orchids (these orchids flower on a very long stem, so the individual heads can be cut off and inserted into orchid phials to give them enough height to suit the design). Such a lovely all-round display would look stunning in a hallway, master bedroom, on a dining room table, or on a low coffee table. The soft-stemmed anemones may need replacing after a few days, but the other blooms should last up to ten days if you keep them in good condition.

HOW TO ARRANGE

1 Place the chicken wire inside the vase and fill the vase with water.

2 Arrange the skimmia stems first. Keep turning the vase around as you add the foliage to create a fully three-dimensional domed effect. Try not to add too much foliage at this stage.

3 Add the single roses next, placing the shorter stems around the edge of the arrangement and longer ones near the centre to reinforce the domed effect. The flowers should look ordered and not muddled. Keep turning the vase so it faces you as you add the roses.

4 Arrange the hypericum and spray roses next, spacing them evenly throughout the arrangement. Recess the flowers slightly so that the tips of the skimmia leaves break the curved contours of the blooms. Then add the anemones.

5 Finally, add the cymbidium orchids – they are quite dominant in this design, so it's worth arranging them last to work out where they sit best.

Flowers and foliage

← 6 white spray roses

↓ 5 cymbidium orchids

↓ 10 hypericum berry stems

6 single → white roses

6 white anemones ↓

← 10 skimmia stems

Other materials

Opaque green glazed flared vase (19cm/7in high)
Chicken wire
Florist's scissors

Possible substitutions

Trachelium (for anemonies), mini amaryllis (for spray roses), Singapore orchids (for cymbidium orchids), berried ivy and rosemary (for skimmia)

ANEMONE TREE

With their richly coloured papery petals, anemones almost look as though they are made out of tissue paper, which helps to give a light, delicate edge to this strong design. This spiral bouquet in floral foam would make a lovely centrepiece on a circular hall or dining room table, or on a mantelpiece or chest of drawers. The anemones will last for five days if you keep the foam moist.

HOW TO ARRANGE

1 Sort the different-coloured anemones into separate piles. Hold an anemone in one hand at the binding point and add one of each colour to it, turning the bunch around slightly in the same direction as you work. Arrange the last flowers at a lower angle around the edges to create a domed effect.

2 Use a length of ribbon that complements the colours of the flowers to tie the arrangement securely. Cut the stems the same length to give an even base.

3 Pack a piece of cellophane or a similar material into the base of the vase to give the anemone stems added height. Place the arrangement in the centre of the vase and insert squares of soaked floral foam around the edges of the vase to wedge the stems in place and keep them upright. The top of the foam should sit 2.5cm (1in) below the rim of the vase. Top the vase up with water and hide the foam with a layer of moss.

INSIDER TIPS

- If moss is difficult to source, cover the pieces of floral foam with mixed, coloured gravel, or shiny black pebbles.

- The anemones will open up and grow a little over time. Although this may make the arrangement a little uneven, it will also add interest and movement to the design.

Flowers and foliage

← 50 mixed anemones

← moss

Other materials

Opaque flared vase (15cm/6in high)
Ribbon
Florist's scissors
Cellophane
1 block floral foam
Craft knife

Possible substitution

Mixed spray roses

AMARYLLIS BOUQUET

This beautiful mixed hand-tied bouquet uses species such as berried ivy as a feature rather than as a backdrop to give structure, definition, and interest. The large amaryllises add variety and colour. The spiral technique is the best way to control the overall shape of these very different blooms. This bouquet is ideal as a gift or as a table centrepiece in a clear glass vase at a dinner party. It will last up to ten days in water if you refresh the water and re-cut the stems.

HOW TO ARRANGE

1 Sort the different ingredients into separate piles. Hold one amaryllis stem gently upright in one hand and encircle it with two or three stems of berried ivy.

2 Add a rose and twist the bunched blooms around slightly in your hand, then add a stem of hypericum. Keep the stems spiralled by adding them all at the same angle and turning the arrangement in the same direction as you work.

3 When you have added one of each of all the different ingredients, check that you are happy with the arrangement of stems by tilting it towards you, or checking it in a mirror. Trim the stems if necessary if the bouquet is becoming unwieldy in your hand. Add another amaryllis stem at an angle and continue to add the rest of the flowers and foliage.

4 Tie the arrangement securely with a length of raffia or garden string. Treat the amaryllis stems with care, as they may split under too much pressure.

5 Cut the stems at an angle so they are roughly the same length and will all be able to sit in water. If the arrangement is well balanced, it should be able to stand unaided. If the bouquet is a gift to someone, stand it in water until you present it.

INSIDER TIP

• Amaryllis stems are fragile and the flower heads they carry are heavy, so the stems can split if held tightly. Buy stems that are as fresh as possible with the buds just opening so the flower heads don't splay out in the arrangement.

Flowers and foliage

← 5 ruby red single roses

↓ 7 'Red Lion' amaryllis

5 'Tamango' spray roses ↓

← 7 'Dolly Parton' hypericum stems

10 berried ivy stems →

Other materials

Florist's scissors
Raffia or garden string

Possible substitutions

Lilies (for amaryllis); eryngium (for spray roses); trachelium (for hypericum); gerberas (for single roses)

WHITE WEDDING

These romantic yet restrained wedding arrangements are deliberately ordered and formal, but with a twist: a mass of tiny frosted pearls are hidden in the buttonhole and bouquet. It's worth showing the bride how to hold her bouquet correctly: its weight should draw her arms down naturally so they are straighter, allowing the flowers to be shown off at the best angle.

BUTTONHOLE

1 stem white spray roses
1 ivy stem
Wired pearls (available from haberdashers, bead shops, and specialist flower markets)

BOUQUET

9 white spray roses
9 white single 'Avalanche' roses
11 white freesias
7 white trachelium
5 white lisianthus
11 eucalyptus stems
Wired pearls (available from haberdashers, bead shops, and specialist flower markets)

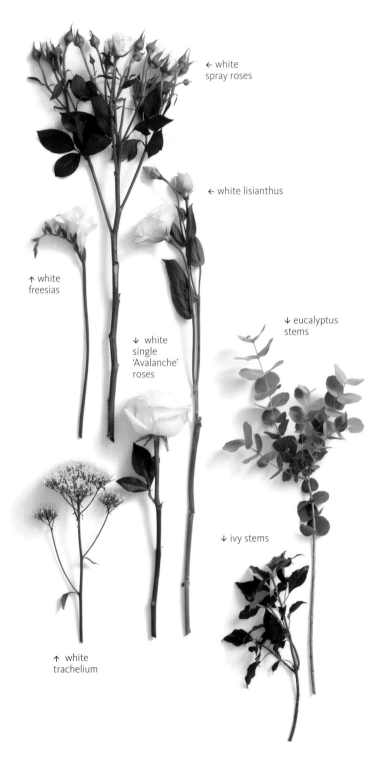

← white spray roses

← white lisianthus

↑ white freesias

↓ eucalyptus stems

↓ white single 'Avalanche' roses

↓ ivy stems

↑ white trachelium

BUTTONHOLE

Sprays of wired pearls tucked in between delicate spray roses are a charming detail that lifts this buttonhole out of the ordinary.

1 Wire the roses and ivy leaves according to the step-by-steps for wiring a buttonhole in section 1 (pp42–45). Gather several wired pearls into a spray and bind the wires together with stem tape.

2 Group the individual roses, arrange the wired pearls around them, and encircle them all with the ivy leaves. Trim the wires so they are graduated, wrap stem tape around all the wires, and press the tape down with your fingers to seal it.

3 Mist the roses occasionally to keep them fresh until they are needed, then supply the buttonhole with a pearl-tipped pin to attach it onto the lapel of a jacket.

BOUQUET

This bouquet is a large spiral-stemmed design with pearls scattered through it. It has a high binding point to give a compact look.

1 Divide the different ingredients into separate piles. Hold a rose and add one of each of the ingredients at an angle to create a spiral effect. Turn the bunch in the same direction as you work, and add lengths of wired pearls.

2 Add all the blooms in turn so that they are balanced equally throughout the bunch. Arrange the last two layers of flowers slightly lower around the edges to create a domed effect.

3 Secure the bunch with a length of raffia or string. Trim the stem ends with secateurs. If you want to cover the stems with ribbon, wind a long length of white ribbon down around the stems and up again. Tie the two ends together in a small knot and press pearl pins in a vertical line into the ribbon to secure it and create a pretty detail. Mist the flowers occasionally until needed.

ORCHID AND ROSE MIX

This luxurious, very full vase arrangement is an all-round (rather than front-facing) display that would look wonderful on a circular table in the centre of a large entrance hall or conservatory. The mix of classical red and silvery green hues is freshened up with exotic pale-pink cymbidium orchids, arching stems of lime-green molucella, and green tie leaves that line the inside of the vase and conceal the stems. Use chicken wire if you find it hard to angle the stems (p31). The flowers will last well for seven to ten days.

HOW TO ARRANGE

1 The central vein, or midrib, of a green tie leaf can break and spoil the visual effect of lining a vase, so use a craft knife or scissors to slice down either side of the midrib of each green tie leaf and separate the leaf into two separate halves. Curl the half-leaves around the inside of the vase in diagonal patterns.

2 Trim the stems of ruscus just a little so that they give height to the display, and arrange them in the vase to create a three-dimensional fan shape. Then add the eucalyptus. To create an all-round arrangement, keep turning the vase around as you work to build up an even shape from every angle.

3 Be aware of the sharp white spikes left on the stems of molucella when you strip off the leaves; cut these spikes off, too, so they don't stand in water. Re-cut the stems just above a join, or node, and arrange them in the centre of the vase, turning the vase around as you work.

4 Arrange the roses next and then the orchids, as they are the most dominant flowers. Place them in the obvious gaps around the arrangement. Check that you have an even, graduated shape from every angle, then put the vase in position and top it up almost to the rim with water.

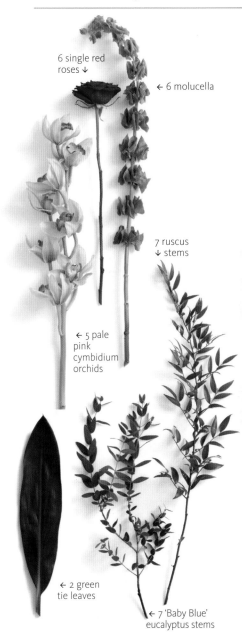

Flowers and foliage

6 single red roses ↓

← 6 molucella

7 ruscus ↓ stems

← 5 pale pink cymbidium orchids

← 2 green tie leaves

← 7 'Baby Blue' eucalyptus stems

Other materials

Flared clear glass vase (30cm/12in high)
Florist's scissors
Chicken wire (optional)

Possible substitutions

Euphorbia (for molucella), amaryllis (for roses), eucalyptus (for ruscus)

EXOTIC ADDITION
Cymbidium orchids with roses may appear an unlikely mix, but the different colours and shapes of these blooms actually enhance one another.

EXOTICS IN A BOX

Exotic flowers and foliage always look sculptural and architectural. To give this hand-tied bouquet a natural feel it is arranged in a wooden box intended to mimic the textural bark of coconut trees. If you prefer to keep to clean lines and smooth surfaces, display the flowers in a glass container, and feel free to choose your own combination of tropical flowers and foliage. This design will look good on a table in a contemporary setting and will last for seven days or so if you keep the flowers in good condition (pp28–29).

HOW TO ARRANGE

1 Take each black tie leaf and make short slashes with a craft knife on either side of the midrib (the central vein running along the length of the leaf blade).

2 Sort the different flowers and foliage into separate piles. Hold a ginger lily in one hand and add an anthurium to it, twisting the stems around slightly in one direction in your hand. Add more stems at the same angle to create a spiral stem effect. Turn the arrangement slightly in the same direction as you work.

3 Leave a few protea stems aside and insert the remaining flowers and foliage at a lower angle around the edges of the bunch to create a domed effect. As you add a black tie leaf, pull the tip of the leaf down to the binding point with one hand so the separated sections curl over. Secure the stems and the tips of the black tie leaves together with raffia.

4 Pack cellophane around the vase in the box to make it secure. Fill the vase with water and place the bunch in it. Add the last few protea around the edges of the vase to echo the square shape of the box and cover the cellophane. Wrap seagrass cord around the box and tie it in a neat knot.

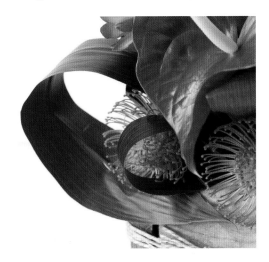

BLACK TIE LEAVES
The three separated sections of this slashed leaf create a ribbon-like effect.

Flowers and foliage

← 5 'African King' anthuriums

← 8 orange and yellow protea

↓ 3 red ginger lilies

1 orange → heliconia

2 umbrella → grass

10 black → tie leaves

Other materials

Wooden box (36 x 36cm/14 x 14in and 25cm/10in deep) with a vase inside
Craft knife
Raffia
Florist's scissors
Cellophane
Seagrass cord

Possible substitutions

Strelitzia (for ginger lilies); Singapore orchids (for protea)

GREEN BOUQUET

With its limited, neutral palette of hues, this hand-tied bouquet suits any room, whether colourful or pristine white. It is also an ideal gift for someone who might prefer a more contemporary arrangement. As it will last well in harsh temperatures such as fierce air-conditioning or hot rooms, it is a suitable choice for the office or a flat. This arrangement will not lose any of its impact if you only use three varieties of green flowers. You could choose all white, red, or pink flowers, too, for an equally vibrant display. The bouquet will last a week if you keep the flowers in good condition (pp28–29).

HOW TO ARRANGE

1 Sort the different flowers and foliage into separate piles. Hold the stem of one flower in your hand and add another variety of flower to it at an angle, twisting the bunch around slightly in one direction in your hand as you do so.

2 Add one of each of all the flowers and leaves at the same angle to create a spiral stem effect, turning the bunch in the same direction as you do so. Reserve most of the green tie leaves until the end. As you add the green tie leaves, fold the tips of the leaves over and hold them at the binding point. This helps to provide an unusual, interesting feature and added texture. Check that you are happy with the arrangement of flowers, then add the remaining blooms. Insert the last two layers of flowers at a lower angle around the edges to create a domed effect, and add the remaining green tie leaves last.

3 Tie the arrangement with garden string or raffia secured in a knot.

4 Cut the stems at an angle, so they are roughly the same length and will all be able to sit in water. If the bouquet is a gift, wrap it and tie it with a black, green, or cream ribbon (pp48–49).

Flowers and foliage

6 shamrock → chrysanthemums

↓15 single roses

↓7 green santini

5 green → anthurium

↑8 green tie leaves

Other materials

Raffia or garden string
Florist's scissors

Possible substitutions

Hydrangeas (for shamrock chrysanthemums); small spray roses (for santini); gerberas (for anthurium)

ORCHID CHAIR-BACK

Simple hand-tied bouquets attached to the back of every chair at a celebration meal make a lovely feature. They can also provide the finishing touches to a special event such as a wedding, Christmas dinner, or summer garden party. This chair-back has been arranged using the spiral hand-tied bouquet technique, but instead of having a domed appearance it is designed to be front-facing, as your guests will view the flowers more often from the front or the side than from above. As the flowers are out of water, they will only last a few hours.

HOW TO ARRANGE

1 Give the orchids a drink, as they will be out of water for the duration of the event. Cut their long stems in the middle to create two separate, short stems.

2 Hold an orchid stem in one hand and add a few stems around it at the binding point. Insert each stem at an angle to create a spiral effect. There is no need to turn the bunch each time, as you want the flowers to all face forwards. Place the longer stems at the back and the shorter stems at the front.

3 Check that you are happy with the arrangement of flowers, then tie them at the binding point with a length of raffia. Cut the ends of the stems straight across to neaten them up.

4 Wrap a long length of ribbon around the top of the chair-back and tie it in a knot at the back. Tie the bouquet onto the ribbon with a short piece of ribbon.

5 Cut one last long piece of ribbon and wrap it around the bouquet at the binding point (to cover the raffia and any visible knots). Secure the ribbon in a bow and allow the loose ends to trail down the back of the chair.

Flowers

6 lime green →
Singapore orchid stems

3 purple →
Singapore orchid stems

STREAMLINED DESIGN
To keep the arrangement aligned with the chair-back, wrap reel wire around a couple of stems and tie the ends onto the chair.

Other materials

Florist's scissors
Raffia
Wide ribbon
Reel wire (optional)

Possible substitution

Spray roses

GERBERA IN LINES

A clean, modern display such as this could be classed as a "perpetual arrangement": the floral foam design is so easy to reinvent that you just pull out the old flowers and insert fresh blooms. Its fun, quirky appearance means that it would suit a kitchen windowsill or hall table, or brighten up the back of a table of food at a children's party. The aim is to create a tiered effect, with the tallest flowers at the back and the shortest at the front, but don't be obsessive about creating exact levels with each row of flowers. It will last for at least a week if you keep the floral foam moist.

HOW TO ARRANGE

1 As the flowers are arranged in foam, stand them in water for an hour or so after trimming their stems. If the container isn't watertight, line it with cellophane or a similar material. Place the soaked, trimmed foam blocks in the container.

2 Trim the stems of four gerberas to similar lengths and press them into the back of the foam so they are equal distances apart. These will be the tallest flowers in the display, so don't cut them too short.

3 Place another row of gerberas, with their stems cut slightly shorter, immediately in front of the first row.

4 Add the last row of gerberas at the front of the arrangement, placing each stem directly in front of the other pairs of gerberas. Then tie each set of tiered stems together with some brightly coloured wire that is preferably the same colour as the flower heads.

5 If you want to add an extra decorative touch to the ties, coil some lengths of wire into swirls (see below). Then scatter enough black pebbles over the surface of the container to completely cover the floral foam.

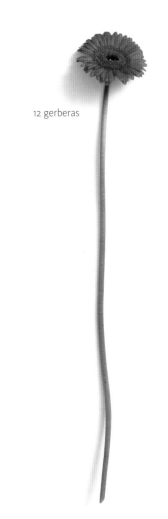

Flowers

12 gerberas

Other materials

Galvanized metal trough
   (41cm/16in long, 15cm/6in deep),
   terracotta trough, or ceramic
   container
Florist's scissors
Cellophane (optional)
1–2 blocks floral foam
Coloured decorative thick
   reel wire
Black pebbles, shells, or gravel

Possible substitution

Anthuriums

DECORATIVE SWIRLS
To make the wire swirls, bend a length of wire (about 3.5cm/1½in) 90° at one end of the wire and pinch and push it into the shape of a loop. Rotate the loop in your fingers to form a circle of wire around it. The circle should be tight enough so that the wires touch, or almost touch. Keep rotating the wire to form six or so circles that together create a swirl. Attach to the front of the stems using the short end of wire at the back of the swirl.

INDEX

ACKNOWLEDGMENTS

ABOUT THE AUTHORS
Mark Welford and Stephen Wicks opened their shop, Bloomsbury Flowers, in London's Covent Garden in 1994. Prior to this, the "Bloomsbury Boys", as they have become known, were dancers with the Royal Ballet. Their mission was to make their arrangements as theatrical as possible but also to keep them simple, classic, and unpretentious.

Bloomsbury Flowers' clients include Firmdale Hotels, with whom they won a silver Grenfell medal at the RHS Chelsea Flower Show in May 2010.

THE AUTHORS WOULD LIKE TO THANK
Our fabulous team at Bloomsbury Flowers especially Megan, Gemma, Janet, Grace, Russ, and Anton.

Susannah Steel for putting our ramblings into coherent text and Jessie for being completely delightful and very patient.

Our wonderful photographer, Carolyn Barber, who is a complete inspiration and a joy to work with.

The team at Dorling Kindersley, including Mary-Clare Jerram for commissioning the book, Caroline de Souza, Dawn Henderson, Christine Keilty, Marianne Markham, Andrew Roff, and William Hicks.

All our suppliers at the New Covent Garden Flower Market as well as MHG Flowers and Metz.

DORLING KINDERSLEY WOULD LIKE TO THANK
Nicky Collings for art directing the photoshoot, Kate Davis for assisting with the photography, Ria Holland for design assistance, Steve Crozier for his retouching work, Sue Morony for proofreading, Marie Lorimer for indexing.

PICTURE CREDITS
All images © Dorling Kindersley
For further information see: www.dkimages.com

! NOTE
Lily pollen is poisonous to cats and dogs, so if you own one, ensure that you remove all the pollen from the lilies before you arrange them.